GARY THOMAS

WITH KEVIN & SHERRY HARNEY

WHEN
TO
WALK
AWAY

STUDY GUIDE | SIX SESSIONS

FINDING FREEDOM
FROM TOXIC PEOPLE

When to Walk Away Study Guide
Copyright © 2019 by Gary Thomas

ISBN 978-0-310-11024-8 (softcover)
ISBN 978-0-310-11025-5 (ebook)

Requests for information should be addressed to: Zondervan, 3900 Sparks Dr. SE, Grand Rapids, Michigan 49546.

Published in association with Yates & Yates, www.yates2.com.

Interior design by InsideOut Creative Arts (insideoutcreativearts.com)

First Printing September 2019 / Printed in the United States of America

HB 03.05.2024

CONTENTS

ACKNOWLEDGMENTS

When we discussed putting together this curriculum, my first choice for the primary writers of the guide were Kevin and Sherry Harney. I never use a writer for my books, as I love the process of writing and even rewriting. Writing books is a joy for me, not a job. But putting together a small-group curriculum is a different format altogether, and I felt that getting two fresh voices to interact with this video curriculum would create a much more helpful guide than trying to do this on my own. Kevin and Sherry had done a fabulous job in writing the *Sacred Marriage Study Guide*, and I thought that if they were available to write this one, too, the end result would be better than trying to do it on my own. When they agreed, it was a very happy day for me.

Months later, when this manuscript came in, I rejoiced to find that Kevin and Sherry had exceeded all my expectations. They have done a fabulous job of making this material accessible, understandable, practical, and helpful. Their experience in ministry shows, and I am so grateful for their gifts on display and the way they can take my words on the screen, a few thoughts from my book, add in their own seasoned perspective and wisdom, and mold all of this into what you now hold into your hands.

Together, the three of us offer this work to God's church, praying that his Spirit will use it to instruct, protect, inspire, guide, and equip his people for the work of his kingdom.

INTRODUCTION

WHAT WOULD YOU DO?

Maria is only ten years old, but she goes to bed with a knot in her stomach and worry in her heart. Her parents notice her joyful spirit only pops up occasionally and she is sullen and moody more and more often. When they ask how she is doing, she gives a quick, "Fine," and avoids any other conversation.

After two months of this pattern getting progressively worse, Maria's parents decide to have a serious conversation with their sweet daughter and let her know they might need to see a family counselor if things don't get better. Confronted with the love and concern of her parents, Maria breaks down in tears. She recounts how her "friend" Holly has been treating her. Lies are being told to the rest of their friend circle. Holly is making threats that Maria will be utterly left out if she does not do whatever Holly says. Maria has asked Holly if she has done something wrong, and Holly has told her that there are all kinds of things wrong with her and she should just be thankful that anyone would play with her.

What would you do if you were Maria's parents? What advice would you give your daughter?

Karl is a transfer student at a new college. After two years of community college and working nights to save money, he is finally attending a great Christian university. This has been his dream from childhood. He is even playing soccer as a walk-on, and the coach saw fit to make him a starting striker. Karl should be having the time of his life. In some ways, he is. He loves his classes and professors. He is amazed that they actually pray to Jesus in many of his classes and faith comes up regularly in his course work and conversations with other students. Karl grew up going to public schools and he is really happy to be in an environment that is warmly welcoming of his Christian faith. But there is a dark cloud hanging over Karl's life and heart.

There are two guys on the soccer team who are relentless in their mocking and unflinchingly cold in their attitude toward him. He knew jumping into a team that had been playing together for a couple years might be awkward. He expected some friendly teasing and a little good-hearted initiation, but this was something entirely different. Most of the guys seemed to like him, but DJ and Johaan were getting crueler as the season went on. Karl tried to build bridges, be nicer, pray for them, and even offered to take them out to dinner and pay the bill. It seemed that the harder he tried to be kind, the more vicious they became. They were even making efforts to turn the other players against Karl.

Karl finally met with his Bible teacher and poured out his heart. He wondered if something was wrong with him. What could he do to get these guys to like him? What had he done wrong? What would you say if you were Karl's Bible teacher?

Toxic people come in all shapes and sizes. We have all met them. Maybe, in our worst moments, we have been them. What we can all agree on is that trying to appease people like Holly, DJ, and Johaan won't improve the situation. In most cases, things will only get worse.

From childhood, to teenage years, to young adulthood, and all through our life, we will face people who are mean, unfair, toxic, and deeply broken. For most of us, we have no category for these people, so we have no idea how to respond. Sometimes we blame ourselves. At other time we try harder to get along and smooth the waters. Those who are compassionate will often pray, care, and try to win them over. Those who are tenderhearted can end up with tears, depression, ulcers, and worse.

In this video Bible study we will look at a topic rarely talked about and often avoided. The fact that you are part of this study says you have courage to tackle the tough stuff in life. By the end of this study you will know what to say to a little girl like Maria, a young man like Karl, to friends and family members when they encounter toxic people. You will even know what to say to yourself when someone like this intersects in your life. Most of all, you will know more about how to love Jesus, stand with your Savior, walk confidently in your mission, and sometimes even walk away from toxic people hand-in-hand with him.

OF NOTE

The quotations interspersed throughout this study guide are excerpts from the book *When to Walk Away: Finding Freedom from Toxic People* and the video curriculum of the same name by Gary Thomas. All other resources including the study introduction, small group questions, session introductions, and between sessions materials have been written by Kevin and Sherry Harney in collaboration with Gary Thomas.

FOLLOW JESUS' EXAMPLE

Jesus walked away from toxic people and let them walk away from him. **We can learn to follow his example.**

INTRODUCTION

For the first fifteen years of their marriage they served the church in two dramatically different ways. Both David and Ginny had gifts for ministry, loved people, and felt honored to serve the same congregation. David was the pastor and Ginny led the music ministry and adult education. Their mission was the same, but they responded to toxic people in totally different ways.

When they started at their first church, a woman came at Ginny like a heat-seeking missile. She was clearly needy and explained to Ginny that she wanted an accountability partner, a friend, a shoulder to cry on, and someone to call (at any time, day or night) when she was in need. This woman was certain that the Lord wanted Ginny to be that person. So, Ginny made the commitment and jumped into a relationship that lasted fifteen long and painful years.

This woman demanded everything and gave nothing back. She would call at all hours and expect Ginny to drop everything, even the care of her children, to listen, pray, and help her manage whatever issue she was facing. When Ginny would try to establish barriers, the woman would declare that Ginny was not loving, not caring, and maybe not even a Christian. She would share this with anyone who would listen.

Over time, this woman began declaring to anyone who would listen that no one at the church cared about her or did anything to help her. She even wrote a letter to the church board saying that Ginny was an unkind person and should not be serving at the church until she learned how to "be more like Jesus." Finally, this angry woman left the church. She told people, "I am going to find a church where the members actually care and where the pastor's wife is not a hypocrite!"

During this same decade and a half, David also encountered a handful of toxic people in their church. He was kind to them but always seemed able to keep them at arm's length. They would make demands of him and he would smile and let them know that it was not his job to be their personal counselor, to meet all of their needs, to be their best friend, or to come to every event they felt he should attend. Some of them got angry and pushed back, but other members of the church would assure David, "That guy has always been like that and everyone knows it!" They would assure him that keeping a safe distance from "that guy" was a wise decision that most of the church members would understand.

Instead of being controlled by a few super-needy, angry, and highly demanding people, David invested that time in two or three leaders each year. He would identify those who were mature leaders that needed some coaching and encouragement and he would pour into them. David also had a gift for finding younger and upcoming leaders and helping them sharpen their gifts, grow in prayer, and learn to serve Jesus in the church and the marketplace.

When David and Ginny accepted a call to move to a new church, they took time to evaluate their ministry. David was thankful that he had the honor of preaching and leading the congregation, but he told Ginny that one of his greatest joys was seeing several leaders take serious steps forward in their love for God, service in the church, and their passion for living out faith in their home and in the workplace. Ginny told David that she celebrated the growth in the music ministry and the adult classes. But, sadly, she had not really invested in developing many leaders. She said, "Most of my time for the last fifteen years has been invested in one woman, and I wonder if I made any lasting impact on her life."

Christians have the tendency of thinking that walking away from anyone or letting anyone walk away from them is a failure on their part.

TALK ABOUT IT

If you or your group members are just getting to know one another, take a few minutes to introduce yourselves. Then, to kick things off, discuss one of the following questions:

- What attitudes and behaviors release a person like David to be fruitful and impactful in ministry and life?

—or—

- What attitudes and behaviors keep a person like Ginny from a full life and ministry?

TEACHING NOTES

As you watch the video teaching segment for this session, use the following outline to record any thoughts or concepts that stand out to you.

NOTES
Greg's story . . . a toxic person in the workplace

An elimination diet . . . this is not just for food

A good offense . . . two keys

Seek first his kingdom

Invest in reliable people

By definition, focusing on some people requires us to occasionally walk away from others.

A good defense . . . know when to walk away

Defining a toxic person . . . let the picture come into focus

Learning from Jesus in the four Gospels . . . watch his example

Sometimes he walked away

He never chased those who walked away

Jesus taught his followers to flee . . . and not feel guilty

Esther's story . . . the fruit of walking away

GROUP DISCUSSION

Take a few minutes with your group members to discuss what you just watched and explore these concepts in Scripture.

1. Tell about a toxic person who has intersected your life. (Be sensitive about using a name or recognizable details in this setting.) How has their behavior and attitudes impacted your life? Would you describe the time you spent with them as "fruitful"? Explain.

2. What is it that causes us to keep playing offense and refuse to walk away from a toxic person? How can being a Christian and looking only at the compassion of Jesus keep a person from walking away?

Sometimes walking away is the best way to defend the good work God is calling us to do.

---

3. What are some of the possible consequences if we refuse to walk away from a toxic person?

Relational consequences:

Spiritual consequences:

Emotional consequences:

Physical consequences:

Tell about how you or someone close to you has faced some of these consequences.

4. Read Matthew 6:33–34. What does it mean to seek God's kingdom above all else (in general and in your own life)? How can following this call of Jesus set the course of our lives (including our relational lives) on the right path?

5. How can the behavior and expectations of a toxic person get in the way of us following this essential call of Jesus for all of his people? How have you seen the pressures of a toxic person keep a sincere Christian (yourself or someone else) from fully following the plans of Jesus?

6. Read 2 Timothy 2:1–2. Inspired by the Holy Spirit, the apostle Paul tells the young pastor Timothy to invest what he is learning into the lives of some reliable and qualified people. Why is it critical that all of us hear this call to invest in a few faithful and receptive people? Who is one person you feel God has placed in your life that you can invest in and help grow deeper in faith, and how can your group members pray for you as you seek to do this?

Toxic people may represent one of Satan's most clever attacks against God's work.

---

7. Read Matthew 8:28–9:1. This crowd could have marveled at the power of Jesus. They could have fallen on their faces and worshiped the Lord of glory. Instead, they asked him to leave their region. Why do you think they responded this way? How did Jesus respond to this request and why do you think he responded this way?

---

*The hearts of some people were not changed
by the actual Messiah when he walked on this earth . . .
so who are we to think that our efforts can fix
every broken person we encounter?*

---

8. Read John 8:58–59 and Matthew 12:13–15. How did Jesus respond in these conflicted and unhealthy situations? How can Jesus be our example when we are around people who are toxic and dangerous? How can walking away be the most godly and honoring thing we can do?

9. Jesus told his followers that there were times and situations where they should flee. Tell about a life situation where you have been "hanging in there," but you believe Jesus might be calling you to walk away. What is keeping you from walking away and what would help you take this step of faith and walk away with Jesus?

CLOSING PRAYER

Spend time in your group praying in some of the following directions:

- Thank God for the faithful people who have taken time to invest in your spiritual journey ,and also pray for those who are still cheering you on as you grow in faith.

- Ask the Holy Spirit to help you recognize and identify people in your life (or the lives of those you love) who are truly toxic. Pray for discernment to know the difference between a difficult person who needs God's care and toxic people who need to be avoided.

- Ask for courage to embrace the idea that one of the godliest things you can do is walk away from toxic people so you have the time and energy to invest in receptive and hungry people.

* Invite your heavenly Father to comfort and care for one of your group members who shared the pain and struggle they have faced because of a toxic person in their life.

Satan knows that he can't stop God's fresh water from flowing through you, so he tries to get you to pour it down the drain of toxic people rather than onto the fertile fields of teachable and thirsty people.

BETWEEN-SESSIONS PERSONAL STUDY

Reflect on the content you've covered this week in *When to Walk Away* by engaging in any or all of the following between-sessions activities. The time you invest will be well spent, so let God use it to draw you closer to him. At your next meeting, share with your group any key points or insights that stood out to you as spent this time with the Lord.

TRY AN ELIMINATION DIET

Some people take time to do an elimination diet with food to see how specific foods are impacting their physical health (and sometimes their emotional health). Try this with a person in your life who you feel might be toxic. Use the process below to guide you:

Pray for wisdom to identify a toxic person. You might already feel you know who that individually is but ask for a confirmation from the Holy Spirit.

Seek wisdom from a confidential, wise, and godly friend or family member. Share what you have experienced in relationship with this person and ask if it sounds like they are operating in a toxic manner. You might want to share some of what you have learned in this study.

Eliminate this person for a set period of time. If they contact you or are around you daily, you might want to make it a week. If they are around weekly, consider making it a month. Either avoid them for this time or let them know that you won't be available for this time period. If they push back strongly, this might be an indicator of the kind of person you are dealing with.

How long I will do this elimination diet: _____

Evaluate how you feel, your emotional condition, your spiritual vitality, and your general outlook during this time. What changes with no contact with the toxic person? Do you feel more peaceful? Does your stress level go down?

OBSERVATIONS:

- _____
- _____
- _____

- _____
- _____
- _____
- _____
- _____

Decide if you need to walk away from this person in some specific and measurable ways. How will you communicate this? Who will pray for you and keep you accountable to follow through?

How I will communicate this decision?

Who will pray for me and keep me accountable to hold to this decision?

LEARNING FROM THE MASTER

Take time in the coming weeks and read all four Gospels. Record when you see Jesus walking away, encouraging his people to walk away, or not chasing after those who walk away from him. Use the space beginning below to record your observations from each of the Gospel accounts of the life and ministry of Jesus.

THE GOSPEL OF MATTHEW (OBSERVATIONS OF JESUS)

Text (Location in the Gospel):	Lesson:

THE GOSPEL OF MARK (OBSERVATIONS OF JESUS)

Text (Location in the Gospel):	Lesson:

THE GOSPEL OF LUKE (OBSERVATIONS OF JESUS)

Text (Location in the Gospel):	Lesson:

THE GOSPEL OF JOHN (OBSERVATIONS OF JESUS)

Text (Location in the Gospel):	Lesson:

After reading all four Gospels, review all of your observations and write down your four biggest composite observations from the life of Jesus recorded in the Bible:

OBSERVATION 1:

OBSERVATION 2:

OBSERVATION 3:

OBSERVATION 4:

FIND RELIABLE AND QUALIFIED PEOPLE

Take time to memorize 2 Timothy 2:2:

> *And the things you have heard me say in the presence of many witnesses entrust to reliable people who will also be qualified to teach others.*

Next, pray for God to place the name or face of one person on your mind. Ask that this person be someone healthy, hungry, and reliable. Ask God to help you invest time and spiritual encouragement in the life of this person.

Decide how you will make this investment and follow through for at least a month. At the end of the month, decide if this is a wise and fruitful use of your time and determine what next steps you will take.

JOURNAL

Use the space provided below and on the following page to write some reflections on the following topics:

- What are the characteristics of those who have poured into my life spiritually and how can I emulate these same traits as I invest in others?

- What are the situations where I have a hard time drawing boundaries and walking away from toxic people? How can I respond in a more Jesus-honoring way in the future and learn to walk away?

- How can I share some of the learning and biblical insight I am gaining from this study with those who are still not aware that Jesus calls us to walk away from toxic people?

RECOMMENDED READING

As you reflect on what God is teaching you through this session, you may want to read chapters 1 and 2 of *When to Walk Away: Finding Freedom from Toxic People.*

RECOGNIZE TOXIC PEOPLE

We need to recognize toxic people so we can walk away, and we need to identify when a person is difficult and not toxic so we don't walk away!

INTRODUCTION

Good dermatologists can look closely at a mole, discoloration on someone's face, or an irritated section of skin and quickly diagnose a potential problem. They can take action that can be life-saving by recognizing squamous cell carcinoma or melanoma and start immediate treatment.

Good dermatologists not only recognize the signs of skin cancer but teach their patients to identify the difference between a skin irritation and a cancerous growth. The best doctors instruct their patients to help themselves (and the doctor) by making wise diagnoses between checkups and quickly getting help when the problem is small and easily treated.

If we are going to deal with toxic people (and we all will), we must learn to make wise diagnoses early in the relationship. When we recognize a toxic person, we can set boundaries, put defenses in place, and walk away in a way that is both firm and as gracious as possible. One key in this process is learning that we will all encounter people who are difficult, irritating, needy, and demanding . . . but who are *not* actually toxic.

We must be careful not to walk away from *every* person who occasionally acts badly, or we will have to walk away from everyone. It is time for us to identify what a toxic person looks like, their patterns, and the consequences we will face if we let them have free reign in our life. At the same time, we can discover how to walk with people who are tough but not toxic.

TALK ABOUT IT

If you or any of your group members are just meeting for the first time, take a few minutes to introduce yourselves and share any insights from last week's personal study. Then, to kick things off, discuss one of the following questions:

- When you think about a person in your life who is difficult and stretches you (but is not toxic), what motivates you to continue interacting with them?

—or—

- What are signs that cause you to wonder if a person has moved beyond being difficult to being a truly toxic individual?

TEACHING NOTES

As you watch the video teaching segment for this session, use the following outline to record any thoughts or concepts that stand out to you.

NOTES
Andrea's story . . . the price we can pay

A little poison goes a long way . . . some gifts are not gifts

Identifying toxic people . . . there are clear indicators

Toxic people can be killers . . . the many ways they murder

•
•
•
•

Rebecca's story . . . still alive, but definitely murdered

---

*Murder is more than wanting someone's
lungs to stop breathing.*

Toxic people can be control mongers . . . Jesus never controlled people

Toxic people love to hate . . . Christians love to love

Toxic people play by different rules . . . they don't care

Discerning the situation . . . ask yourself these questions

-
-
-
-
-
-

A caveat . . . the story of Paul and Silas

Toxic people will take you down, destroy your mission, deflate your enthusiasm, drive you crazy, and make you feel guilty, shameful, and discouraged.

GROUP DISCUSSION

Take a few minutes with your group members to discuss what you just watched and explore these concepts in Scripture.

1. What were some of the costs and consequences for Andrea because she spent most of her first year of college in such close proximity to a toxic person?

   Physically:

   Relationally:

   Emotionally:

Spiritually:

Academically:

Other costs:

How does this story give us a window into the sinister and powerful damage that a toxic person can cause?

2. What are some of the potential dangers of being overly "nice" to a toxic person and trying to "get along" for the sake of keeping the peace?

3. What are some common ways you navigate the relational challenges of a difficult person? Why do our "normal" relational strategies not work with a toxic person?

4. What are some things a toxic person does that act like small drops of poison? Why is it essential to get completely away from a toxic person (at least for a season)?

5. Read John 8:42–44 and Matthew 5:21–22. Murder is more than killing a person physically. The enemy of our soul, Satan, is a murderer and delights in our destruction. What are some of the ways a toxic person can murder or kill (without actually physically killing a person)?

Toxic people wnat you to stop doing what you believe God created you to do.

---

6. What are some possible signs or indicators that a person is trying to murder one of these? What are tactics you have seen a toxic person use?

Your joy . . .

Your peace . . .

Your reputation . . .

Your productivity . . .

Your vocation . . .

Some other area of your life . . .

7. **Read Revelation 3:20 and 1 Corinthians 14:29–33.** God cares about order, but he is not controlling or manipulative. How do toxic people seek to control others, and why is this so opposed to the will and ways of Jesus?

8. Read Colossians 3:5–17. Toxic people love to hate. What does Paul say about the character and actions of an ungodly (and often toxic) person in this passage?

People growing in Christ's love to love. What does this passage say about the heart of a person who is seeking to live like and for Jesus?

9. Being nice to a toxic person or trying to placate them rarely removes the venom of their behavior. Tell about a time when you unwisely interacted with a toxic person and faced negative consequences accordingly.

In retrospect, what would you have done differently in this relationship?

If your beliefs make a toxic person feel guilty, they want to remove your voice and influence.

10. Read Acts 16:22–31. When others are toxic, we are tempted to be mean, retaliatory, or even toxic in response to their behavior. What do you learn from Paul and Silas in this passage when it comes to responding to toxic people and circumstances? How did God use their mature and godly response to a toxic situation?

How can your group members pray for you and support you as you seek to respond to a toxic relationship in a God-honoring way?

CLOSING PRAYER

Spend time in your group praying in some of the following directions:

- Ask the Holy Spirit to give you wisdom and discernment to know when you are dealing with a toxic person (that you should walk away from) or a difficult person (who needs you to extend care).

- Pray for group members who are healing from the attacks and collateral damage of being around a toxic person for a long time.

- Ask God to grow his grace, love, and care in you so that you can be a conduit of his presence to others.

- Pray for power (for each of your group members) not to retaliate or become negative (or even toxic) in response to the bad behavior of others.

God's servants need to know the markers of a toxic person so they can avoid being spiritually assaulted and poisoned by them.

BETWEEN-SESSIONS PERSONAL STUDY

Reflect on the content you've covered this week in *When to Walk Away* by engaging in any or all of the following between-sessions activities. The time you invest will be well spent, so let God use it to draw you closer to him. At your next meeting, share with your group any key points or insights that stood out to you as spent this time with the Lord.

DIFFICULT OR TOXIC?

We will all encounter people who are difficult. They might demand a little too much from us. They can be awkward when it comes to personal space and boundaries. They might even be irritating. These people need love, care, and patience.

We don't have to meet all of their needs, but God will often call us to minister to them. These are not toxic people; they are just difficult.

Then there are toxic people. They are killers. Joy wilts in their presence. They delight in seeing our dreams die and our confidence crushed. Toxic people are dangerous and must be avoided or removed from our lives. We can't help or fix these people because they refuse to change and actually seem to enjoy causing harm to others.

Take a few minuites to make a list of some of the characteristics of difficult people. What are they like? What do they do? How do they act? what do they want from you? Then, think about why they do what they do.

Difficult People: What They Do . . .	Why They Do It . . .

What are appropriate ways to interact with and respond to these people?

- _____
- _____
- _____
- _____
- _____

Now take time to make a list of some of the characteristics and behaviors of toxic people. What are they like, what do they do, how do they act, what do they want from us? Then, think about why they do what they do.

Toxic People: What They Do . . .	Why They Do It . . .

What are necessary ways to walk away from these people, build barriers, and contain the damage they bring?

- _____
- _____
- _____
- _____
- _____

Use these lists to help you identify toxic people and set a strategy for keeping them from harming you.

BE A SHERLOCK HOLMES

Look back at a relationship you had with a toxic person. Maybe you never knew what to call them (toxic) and maybe you never realized what you were dealing with until just now. But this person has run wild in your life with the heart and behavior of a murderer. Look back and name the ways they have damaged your life. What did they murder or try to kill? Where did they succeed and where were you protected? Identify what happened so you can be sure it never happens again.

OBSERVATION #1: WHAT DID THIS PERSON MURDER OR TRY TO MURDER IN ME?

What it was:

What they did and how it impacted me:

How I am still feeling the pain and cost of their actions:

OBSERVATION #2: WHAT DID THIS PERSON
MURDER OR TRY TO MURDER IN ME?

What it was:

What they did and how it impacted me:

How I am still feeling the pain and cost of their actions:

OBSERVATION #3: WHAT DID THIS PERSON
MURDER OR TRY TO MURDER IN ME?

What it was:

What they did and how it impacted me:

How I am still feeling the pain and cost of their actions:

Again, be sure to use these revelations to help you identify
when another toxic person has snuck into your life. Read
about the impact they had on you and make a decision to
never let someone do this to you in the future.

KNOW THE MENU

In Colossians 3:5–9, writes, "Put to death, therefore, whatever
belongs to your earthly nature: sexual immorality, impurity,
lust, evil desires and greed, which is idolatry. Because of these,
the wrath of God is coming. You used to walk in these ways,
in the life you once lived. But now you must also rid yourselves of all such things as these: anger, rage, malice, slander,
and filthy language from your lips. Do not lie to each other."

What are some of the behaviors and attitudes in this passage that give you a picture of what drives a toxic person?

- _____
- _____
- _____
- _____
- _____
- _____
- _____
- _____

Watch for these characteristics in the people around you who seem to be acting in a toxic way. When you see them, prepare to watch closely and be ready to walk away if this person is treating you in ways that are toxic.

JOURNAL

Use the space provided on the next page to write some reflections on the following topics:

- Why I need to love and stay connected to difficult people? How can God actually grow me and make me stronger by loving and serving these people?

- How do toxic people impact a home, family, church, and circle of friends?

- How will I respond the next time I have a clear sense that I am interacting with a toxic person?

RECOMMENDED READING

As you reflect on what God is teaching you through this session, you may want to read chapters 3–5 of *When to Walk Away: Finding Freedom from Toxic People.*

BUILD A GOOD OFFENSE

God has given you a mission to seek his kingdom first and maximize your life, time, and gifts for his glory. To do this, you have to stay focused on your calling and walk away from toxic people . . . over and over again.

INTRODUCTION

The same story with two dramatically different endings.

Esther is a committed and tenderhearted Christian woman who tries to live like Jesus in both the big and small things of life. She and her husband were married for forty-two wonderful years and raised two kids together, and then rejoiced to welcome four grandchildren into their growing family. Two years ago, after a sudden and massive heart attack, Esther's husband passed away. Now she is navigating a new season of life.

Gertrude started coming to the church Esther attends just six months ago. She reached out to Esther because, as Gertrude was fond of saying, "We are in the same boat. We are partners in suffering!" Gertrude had told Esther, and anyone else who would listen, that she had left her last two churches because no one cared for her, the pastors never called on her, and most of the people in those churches were very selfish and not really filled with the Holy Spirit in the way that she was.

Esther saw some red flags with Gertrude's constant complaining and critical attitude, but she also felt bad for her loss of a husband and the pain she felt over so many people failing to care for her and meet her needs.

Take #1—Esther decided she would help Gertrude find some joy in life. She would love Gertrude so much that she would forget the pain of the long list of pastors and church members who had selfishly ignored her needs. Esther spent time with Gertrude almost daily. On the occasional days Esther was busy helping with her grandkids all day, Gertrude would call three or four times to let Esther know how lonely she was and how concerned she was for Esther's spiritual condition. She did not think Jesus would like the fact that Esther was apathetic toward the needs of "her closest friend."

Esther tried to launch a grief support group and did all she could to include Gertrude in the process. The problem was that Gertrude dominated the group by always talking about her problems and never listened to the others. When someone would share his or her pain, loss, or struggle, Gertrude would always tell a story that made it sound like her pain was worse than anyone else's. The group started with six women and two men. After just two months, it was just Esther and Gertrude. Esther was deeply hurt when Gertrude told her (and a few other people) that no one wanted to be in the group because Esther was not a very good leader and lacked compassion for those in need. Gertrude let people know that she was only staying in the group because she felt sorry for Esther.

Take #2—Esther really cared about Gertrude's pain and struggles, but she was also cautious because Gertrude had so many bad things to say about other churches, pastors, and Christians. Esther called the pastor of the most recent church that Gertrude had left and let him know that Gertrude was now attending her church. The pastor was kind, cautious, and tried to be gracious. But he gave Esther a warning to be very careful about letting Gertrude lead any ministry and alluded to the fact that there was a need to repair some of the heartache and pain she brought to those who sought to be her friend. Esther asked if the pastor had ever visited Gertrude. He let out a soft chuckle. "We have two pastors at our church and we both called on her more than anyone else in the church. But, it never seemed to be enough."

After calling both churches Gertrude had attended and having very similar conversations with the pastors, Esther decided to walk away. She told Gertrude that her schedule would be very full because she would be investing in her two kids, their spouses, and her four grandchildren. She would also be starting a new ministry at the church. With all the work she felt the Lord was calling her to do in this season of her life, she simply did not have the margin to be spending lots of time hanging out with Gertrude.

In a matter of weeks Gertrude had written lots of very angry letters to Esther, the church board, and to the pastor explaining why she would be leaving the church. In a matter of months, Esther was leading a thriving group of fifteen people who were ministering to each other and extending the grace of Jesus in their journey through grief. Because she had set healthy boundaries, she had time to prepare for this group, lead it, and invest in a number of dear women who were living with some real challenges. This brought Esther deep joy as she could see God using her in both her family and in her new ministry.

Understanding our mission before God will go a long way toward helping us to sidestep toxic people.

TALK ABOUT IT

Begin your group time by inviting anyone to share his or her insights from last week's personal study. Next, to kick things off, discuss one of the following questions:

- Why are we quick to embrace toxic people, and what tactics do they use to draw us in?

—or—

- Why is it important to draw boundaries with toxic people, and how do they respond when we do this?

Putting our best efforts into reliable people is a biblical call, not a preference.

TEACHING NOTES

As you watch the video teaching segment for this session, use the following outline to record any thoughts or concepts that stand out to you.

Jessica's story... challenging family dynamics

A Civil War story . . . "There is no time for that!"

Seek first God's kingdom . . . this is urgent

If you're in Christ, you aren't just saved;
you're enlisted. Your time isn't your own.

Avoid building false kingdoms . . . there are plenty of options

Invest in reliable people . . . this is God's call

More lessons from Jessica's story . . . value of wise counsel

Joseph's blessing . . . don't waste your arrows

Investing in reliable people . . . always better than being slowed down by toxic people

GROUP DISCUSSION

Take a few minutes with your group members to discuss what you just watched and explore these concepts in Scripture.

1. How will things change in our relationship to toxic people when we look at their demands and the pressure they put on us through the mission of Jesus instead of through the guilt and shame they try to pile on us?

The Holy Spirit within us is so powerful and the work of building the kingdom of God is so necessary that we don't have time to waste on toxic people.

---

2. Read John 9:4 and Matthew 6:33. Respond to this statement: Following the mission that Jesus gives us is so important that we absolutely cannot let the distractions and discouragement of toxic people get in our way. Tell about how a toxic person has brought distraction, discouragement, or even depression to your life.

When you wake up, what drives you? What is first on your agenda? What is your first concern?

---

3. Tell about a person you know who puts God's kingdom first in their life. How do they keep their focus on what matters most to God and how does this impact and guide their decisions each day?

4. Read 2 Timothy 4:5. Timothy is called to endure hardship. This is part of the life of a follower of Jesus. What are some of the hardships and difficulties you might face if you push back against a toxic person? As bad as these consequences are, how can failing to walk away from this toxic person lead to worse consequences?

5. Read 2 Corinthians 5:14–15. Christ died so we can share in his mission of bringing heaven to earth. Make a short list of some of your callings (e.g., being a son or daughter, spouse, parent, grandparent, friend, employee, employer, neighbor). What are some ways that heaven comes to earth when you fulfill your calling? If you do not fulfill your God-given calling because a toxic person is beating you down and consuming your energy and time, what things might never happen through your life?

6. What are some of the less important kingdoms we can be tempted to spend our time building? Why do we need to make sure none of these pursuits (and many of these are not bad) do not become the central focus of our lives?

7. Read 2 Timothy 2:2. Tell about a faithful person who has invested in your spiritual journey and growth over the years. How has their investment impacted you, and how did God use them to make you who you are today?

Life isn't about obtaining personal comfort and eternity. It's about fulfilling your divine mission on earth.

8. How can living a full life following and serving Jesus act as an antidote to letting toxic people take over our schedules, consume our minds, and burden our hearts? What are steps you can take to be sure your life is full and invested in the kingdom things that matter most?

9. We all need a person in our lives who has spiritual wisdom and can speak truth to us, even when we might resist it. For Jessica, it was Adrian. Adrian gave Jessica perspective, encouragement, and spoke heavenly truth. Who in your life plays this sort of a role and how might they help you determine if toxic people are keeping you from being fruitful for Jesus?

Don't let a toxic person slow you down, even for a second. There is no time for that!

10. Who is a reliable person in your circle of influence who you can pour time, prayer, encouragement, and love into so that he or she grows in faithfulness to Jesus and is equipped to help other people grow in faith? What steps can you take in the coming month to invest in this relationship and help this person on his or her journey of spiritual growth?

The Christian life embraces mission. You've been called to something bigger, more glorious, and ultimately far more fulfilling than building your own kingdom.

CLOSING PRAYER

Spend time in your group praying in some of the following directions:

- Lift up a prayer of thanks for a person in your life who has been a model of seeking first God's kingdom and will for his or her life.

- Pray for courage to put God's kingdom first in your life no matter what the cost. Ask God to grow your love for his will so much that the demands of toxic people will seem small and easy to reject.

- Ask the Holy Spirit to give you the discipline and commitment to find a reliable person to invest in and to take the time to pour into his or her life.

- Ask for God to help you see the potential consequences that might come if you do not walk away from a toxic person in your life.

- Pray for your church to know how to deal with people who are toxic and bringing damage to your church leaders, congregation, or reputation.

- Thank God for the fruit he has grown in your life and the things he has done through you because, at some time in the past, you set a boundary and walked away from a toxic person.

One of the big reasons we limit our exposure to toxic people is because we are devoted to growing God's church.

BETWEEN-SESSIONS PERSONAL STUDY

Reflect on the content you've covered this week in *When to Walk Away* by engaging in any or all of the following between-sessions activities. The time you invest will be well spent, so let God use it to draw you closer to him. At your next meeting, share with your group any key points or insights that stood out to you as spent this time with the Lord.

ENDURING HARDSHIP FOR A BETTER FUTURE

Every person on earth will face hardship at one time or another. The real question to ask is *what kind* of hardship you will have to endure during your time in this world.

Make a list of some of the specific hardships that you could face if you actually chose to walk away from a specific toxic person in your life:

Next, make a list of some of the hardships you might experience if you *don't* walk away from this same person:

Pray for courage and power to walk away and endure the hardships that come rather than living with the consequences of staying in a toxic relationship. Write your prayer below.

GROWING URGENT!

God has given you a mission—a calling in this world. As a matter of fact, most of us have more than one. We are all called to use our gifts to serve Jesus and his church, be a good friend, and share the love of Jesus with those who are far from him. Some are called to a marriage relationship. Others are called to be parents or grandparents. Many have vocational callings. The list goes on and on.

Think about two callings that you have. What good things can happen if you are faithful to each of these callings?

My calling:

Good things God can do through this calling:

Next, make a list of what could be lost or missed if you don't realize your calling because you are distracted, discouraged, or depressed because you let a toxic person poison your life.

Ask God to help you remember this second list when you are deciding if it is time to walk away from a toxic person.

FOCUSING ON FINDING RELIABLE PEOPLE

Pray for God to help you identify one or two reliable people he might want you to invest in.

PERSON #1:

PERSON #2:

Look around your church, neighborhood, the homes of family members, and other places you go regularly. Keep your eyes and heart open. Keep asking God to lead you to a reliable person you can pour your life into.

Ask people you trust and respect about who they feel you might invest time, care, and love in. This could be through a one-on-one relationship or in a ministry of some sort.

Try spending time with this person to see if both you and this other person have a sense that God might be opening the door for a relationship that includes some spiritual mentoring and encouragement.

Formalize this relationship by volunteering for a ministry (working with children or youth in the church is a great way to do this) or agreeing with someone that you will meet with some kind of agreed-upon regularity for spiritual encouragement and growth.

JOURNAL

Use the space provided below to write some reflections on the following topics:

- Why do I let toxic people impact and influence my life after I recognize what is happening?

- How can my life have greater impact for the kingdom of God if I learn to have a better defense when it comes to toxic people?

- What are my next steps that will help me walk away from toxic people?

RECOMMENDED READING

As you reflect on what God is teaching you through this session, you may want to read chapters 6 and 7 of *When to Walk Away: Finding Freedom from Toxic People.*

CREATE A GOOD DEFENSE

*You will encounter toxic people. Get to know their tactics, patterns, and motivation . . . **then mount your defense** and walk away so you can do what God has planned for you.*

INTRODUCTION

What if you knew your opponent's game plan? What if you were able to study their plan of attack and be ready for whatever they were going to throw at you? Just imagine the defense you could put in place if you only knew when and how your enemy was going to attack.

There is a reason professional and college sports teams study the film of their opponent's past games. There are actually staff people hired to dissect the offense of a team so that they can prepare their defense for maximum effectiveness. A loss or a victory can hang in the balance.

Now, imagine if you knew the tactics, game plan, and strategies of toxic people. How would that help your life? What if you knew the most common behaviors and attitudes of toxic people so you could be ready before they attack? Imagine the pain you could avoid, the wasted time you would save, and the heartache you would circumvent.

Here is the great news. There is a wonderful book in the Old Testament that gives us vivid detail about the offensive attacks of toxic people. This book also lifts up an example of a leader and a group of faithful people who put in place an effective defense that stood strong against the attacks of toxic people.

Imagine how successful a sports coach would be if he or she had the playbook of the opposing team before the game even started. Today, we will look at the "playbook" of the toxic people in our lives and take time preparing our defense for the next time we meet.

Dealing with toxic people requires laser sharp focus with wisdom, discernment, and determination.

TALK ABOUT IT

Begin your group time by inviting anyone to share his or her insights from last week's personal study. Next, to kick things off, discuss one of the following questions:

• What are some of the main tactics you have noticed that toxic people will use against you or the people you care about?

—*or*—

• What are strategies you have seen used or have used to set up a defense against the tactics of a toxic person?

In most places we live or work, toxic people are there and sometimes they will come after us.

TEACHING NOTES

As you watch the video teaching segment for this session, use the following outline to record any thoughts or concepts that stand out to you.

Alicia's story . . . an overwhelming coworker

Sometimes you can't just walk away . . . so practice wisdom

The tactics of toxic people . . . both blatant and passive

To be given a mission from God means we will be surrounded by opponents and toxic enemies.

Nehemiah's story . . . a powerful example

Getting the historical context

Some insights about toxic people:

- They lie

- They make threats

- They enlist others

- They gossip

- They want you off God's mission

- They want you on their program (mission)

- They pretend to be your friend

- They intimidate

- They shame

- They play the religious card

The best way to overcome toxic people . . . stay focused on God's mission

The results when we resist toxic people . . . amazing!

The end result of Nehemiah's focus, determination, and adept handling of toxic opposition is a stunning and stupendous victory. It can be for you too!

GROUP DISCUSSION

Take a few minutes with your group members to discuss what you just watched and explore these concepts in Scripture.

1. Tell about a toxic person you were simply not able to walk away from because of the unique relationship (family member, coworker, neighbor, etc.). How did you set up

barriers and boundaries even when you could not fully sever the relationship? How did they respond?

2. Respond to this statement: *If we have been given a mission from God, we will be surrounded by toxic and clever enemies. The bigger the mission, the more toxic the enemy.*

3. What are blatant and frontal attacks that toxic people can make? What are subtle and passive acts of aggression made by toxic people?

4. Read Nehemiah 4:1–18 and 6:1–15. Make a list of the attacks and tactics of Nehemiah's enemies. What did they do? What was behind their toxic behavior?

TACTIC #1:

What these toxic people were trying to do:

How toxic people still use this tactic today:

TACTIC #2:

What these toxic people were trying to do:

How toxic people still use this tactic today:

TACTIC #3:

What these toxic people were trying to do:

How toxic people still use this tactic today:

Distracting you is a win for a toxic person. If they can't ultimately defeat your work, they will try to delay it.

5. How did Nehemiah and the people of God respond to the toxic attacks, and what defenses did Nehemiah set up to be prepared to stand against these attacks? What do you learn from his attitudes and actions?

How can you adopt one of these defensive behaviors?

6. When you look at the tactics of Nehemiah's toxic detractors, how are people using those same destructive strategies today? What are defensive measures we can take to fortify ourselves so that we don't get pulled away from the mission and task God has placed before us? (Work as a group and try to come up with at least ten practical defensive strategies.)

- _____
- _____
- _____
- _____

- _____
- _____
- _____
- _____
- _____
- _____

> *When a toxic person doesn't get his or her way, that person will often resort to trying to make you look and sound sinister.*

7. Toxic people hunger for attention and cry out for our time. But instead of giving in to their demands, we need to commit ourselves to pray more. Rather than wasting our time talking with toxic people, we can invest our time in talking with God. How does prayer strengthen us and carry us through battles with toxic people?

> *Church people can be just as toxic as non-church people.*

8. One of the most sinister things that toxic people can do is bring their attack under the guise of religion. How can toxic people spiritualize their attacks, and what can we do to defend ourselves against this?

9. **Read Nehemiah 6:16.** How can God be glorified when we determine to establish a strong defense against the attacks of toxic people? How does our robust and godly defense actually serve and help a toxic person more than us giving in to their desires and demands?

10. **Read Nehemiah 8:6 and Nehemiah 13:31.** What are some of the blessings and amazing results that can come when we refuse to let toxic people have their way and rule our lives, homes, workplaces, churches, or any part of our world? Tell a story of how God did something productive, fruitful, amazing, or surprising after you walked away from a toxic person.

CLOSING PRAYER

Spend time in your group praying in some of the following directions:

- Take a few minutes for silent prayer as a group. Look at the list of the tactics and behaviors of a toxic person (in the video outline earlier in this session). Be honestly humble and ask if any of those patterns are growing or popping up in your life. If you recognize them, even in a small way, confess these to God and ask God to remind you of his grace. Pray for power to change your attitudes and behavior in this area.

- Ask the Holy Spirit to give you discernment when you encounter a toxic person. Pray that you will see their tactics and attacks for what they are, so you can prepare a robust defense.

- Thank God for biblical teaching and stories that reveal the tactics of toxic people. Pray that you learn from these clear biblical lessons.

- Pray for courage to act on your defensive plan, and then to act on it again until it becomes lifestyle.

Toxic people sound reasonable, but mission-minded people don't have time for sentimental foolishness.

BETWEEN-SESSIONS PERSONAL STUDY

Reflect on the content you've covered this week in *When to Walk Away* by engaging in any or all of the following between-sessions activities. The time you invest will be well spent, so let God use it to draw you closer to him. At your next meeting, share with your group any key points or insights that stood out to you as spent this time with the Lord.

AM I GETTING TOXIC?

Take time some for self-examination. Read through the toxic behaviors and tactics listed below. Then, read Nehemiah chapters four and six. Look at all the behaviors, motives, and actions of the enemies of Nehemiah. Ruthlessly examine your life and relationships and ask yourself if you see any of these in the way you treat others . . . even a little bit.

Do I see any signs of this in me?

- Lying
- Making threats
- Enlisting others to be on my side
- Gossiping
- Distracting others from what God wants them to do
- Pretending to be someone's friend
- Intimidating others
- Placing shame on others
- Playing the religious card

Some changes I need to make to keep toxic patterns and behaviors out of my heart and life:

Pray for the power of the Holy Spirit to fill you so that you can resist the temptation to be toxic, even in small ways.

PRACTICE MAKES PERFECT!

If you have a toxic person in your life and have identified their tactics and patterns (over weeks, months, or years) but have still not confronted them or set boundaries that allow you to walk away from their influence, try this exercise.

1. **Find a mature, godly, and confidential friend.** Share what you have been experiencing in this toxic relationship and what it is doing to you. Explain the offensive attacks this toxic person uses and be detailed. Name their tactics.

2. **Pray with your friend.** Pray for power to resist these attacks and ask God to help you develop a defense against the actions of this toxic person.

3. **Develop your defense together.** What will you say the next time this person treats you in their toxic manner? How will you respond? What will "walking away" look like? How can you be gracious but firm?

4. **Role-play your responses to the toxic person.** Have your friend speak to you or treat you just like the toxic person does (by now you have coached them and explained how the toxic person acts). Then, give your response. Seek to be as clear and direct as you hope to be the next time you encounter the toxic person.

5. **Evaluate how it went.** Let your trusted friend tell you how you can sharpen and develop your response to be

clear, strong, and as kind as possible while still speaking exactly what you need to speak.

6. **Practice again.** Do this role-play exercise and receive feedback until you feel ready to face the toxic person in your life.

7. **Pray together for the leading of the Holy Spirit.** Pay also for courage to face this toxic person with a well-planned defense that is practiced and ready.

8. **Meet with your trusted friend.** After you encounter the toxic person and express all you have prepared, meet with your trusted friend for a time of debriefing and prayer. If there is another toxic situation with the same person, or some other person, walk through steps 2 through 8 again.

LEARN FROM NEHEMIAH

Read the book of Nehemiah. Use the space provided to write down your observations of the following:

What do I learn about the hearts, motives, and behaviors of toxic people as I read about Nehemiah's enemies?

What do I learn about resisting toxic people, standing strong, and formulating an effective defense as I read about Nehemiah and the people of God?

What do I learn about God's presence, power, and work as I read the book of Nehemiah?

JOURNAL

Use the space provided below to write some reflections on the following topics:

- How can I step up, live with greater boldness, and develop a strong defense against the toxic people who come my way?

- What are some of the common tactics toxic people seem to use with me?

- How can I be ready to defend against these the next time I encounter a toxic person?

RECOMMENDED READING

As you reflect on what God is teaching you through this session, you may want to read chapter 10 of *When to Walk Away: Finding Freedom from Toxic People.*

SPEAK THE TRUTH

Speaking the truth means calling a toxic person toxic. We pay a great price when we fail to speak the truth about toxic people. We label people with humility and care, remembering that Jesus also labeled toxic people.

INTRODUCTION

Chip and Bethany stop at a Mexican restaurant where they have never eaten before. It has great ratings online and the reviews say, "Very Authentic." When the waiter brings chips to the table, he sets down three different bowls of hot sauce. Cindy is impressed and happy that the bowls are actually marked MILD, HOT, and VERY HOT (with a fun little picture of flames). Bethany loves Mexican food, but she has burned her taste buds too many times at places that have not given a clear warning about how spicy their salsa is. On the way out of the restaurant after dinner Bethany asks if she can talk with the manager. She enthusiastically says, "I really appreciated the clear labels and the warning on the extra-hot sauce. Nice touch!"

THIN ICE! DANGER! Ernesto posted five different signs with these words in red paint along the edge of the pond on the far corner of his property at the beginning of every winter. Even though most of the ponds around town would freeze enough for the kids to play hockey, his pond had a natural spring that fed into it all year long. He knew the ice was never quite thick enough to be truly safe, even though it looked fine to the casual observer. When his new neighbors moved in, they thought Ernesto was just being protective of his land and pond and was trying to keep their five kids off "his pond." When his new neighbors came over and asked Ernesto if their kids could skate on the pond, they had a great conversation and discovered that he was actually posting the signs to protect the kids in the neighborhood . . . including theirs.

"This product contains traces of peanuts and peanut oil." Ben had often made jokes about what he called the "silly warning labels" companies put on their products. He had causally joked about parents and kids who were "afraid of a peanut" as he put it. Now, just four years later, Ben read every food label religiously.

You see, his daughter Amelia was born with severe allergies of many kinds, including peanut allergies. He had been in the hospital twice when she had a reaction and one time he almost lost Amelia due to a severe response to food she did not know had peanuts in it. Ben was so thankful for the warning labels and frustrated with those who did not see the need to post this kind of warning. It was no longer a laughing matter.

Warning labels and signs are everywhere. Bridge out. Falling rocks. Poison. Bio hazard. Wet paint. Video surveillance in use. Beware of dog. High voltage. The list goes on and on. What all these labels or warning signs have in common is that they exist to help and protect us. If we ignore them, we do so at our own peril!

Healing and understanding in our relatioships comes from telling the truth about one another.

TALK ABOUT IT

Begin your group time by inviting anyone to share his or her insights from last week's personal study. Next, to kick things off, discuss one of the following questions:

- What are some of the consequences we might face **if we ignore posted warnings or labels?**

—*or*—

- Tell about a time that you were saved, protected, or avoided harm because of a well-posted warning.

It might shock you to know that Jesus and his disciples often used labels on the path of ministry.

TEACHING NOTES

As you watch the video teaching segment for this session, use the following outline to record any thoughts or concepts that stand out to you.

Vanessa's story . . . call it what it is

Pigs and dogs . . . what is this all about?

Hard truth . . . what is Jesus saying about how we relate to some people?

Time for triage . . . making hard decisions

Spiritual discernment . . . *no conviction, no counsel*

When you embrace a toxic person instead of walking away, they'll often insult you, hate you, attack you, and abuse you. Jesus wants to spare you from that.

Tim's story . . . dealing with selfishness and manipulation

Labels . . . tough, but sometimes necessary and helpful

Be careful . . . don't give labels too quickly or lightly

GROUP DISCUSSION

Take a few minutes with your group members to discuss what you just watched and explore these concepts in Scripture.

1. Why should we be cautious about putting a label like "toxic" or "abusive" on a person?

What are some of the dangers and consequences if we use these kinds of labels lightly or wrongly?

2. Read Matthew 7:6. How is this verse a powerful call to truth telling? What does Jesus mean when he calls people dogs and swine, and what specific warning is he giving to his followers?

Jesus warns his followers you can give some people the best truth and care, but they simply won't appreciate it.

3. Jesus is clear that there are some people we should not invest our energy and spiritual capital into. Their lives, attitudes, and behaviors make it unwise and even dangerous for us to minister to these people. What are some specific attitudes and behaviors that help you realize you are facing one of the kinds of people Jesus refers to as "dogs" and "pigs"?

4. Jesus warns us that these people will actually turn on us, attack us, and try to "tear us to pieces." What are some of the ways these people seek to attack and harm those who speak the truth to them?

If you have come under this kind of attack, what did you experience? How did it feel? In light of this experience, how do the words of Jesus in Matthew 7:6 ring true?

5. Read 1 Corinthians 2:14, Matthew 9:37–38, and Proverbs 9:7–9. Each of us needs to make decisions about how we will invest our time, words, and ministry into other people. Respond to this statement: *"One of the best ways to make sure we are making the wisest investment of our lives is identifying if a person is toxic and refuse to pour any more time or energy into them."*

What are some of the reasons we might be tempted to keep investing care, time, and energy into a toxic person, even after we realize who they are?

We want to think the best of everyone, but if we don't tell the truth with an accurate label, we can't get to the root issue. We risk harming ourselves.

6. What are some of the dangers of using labels with people who are behaving in a toxic or abusive way? Why is it important that we still use labels with these kinds of people, even when it might make us uncomfortable?

7. Read Matthew 23:29, 33 and Acts 13:9–10. Jesus labeled people *dogs, pigs, a fox, fools, hypocrites, blind guides, snakes, vipers,* and more. The apostle Paul followed suit and used deeply revealing and harsh titles for people who were clearly working against the will of God. How are using labels when dealing with toxic people actually an act of truth and honoring to God? If we fail to do this, how are we resisting the truth and working against God?

The fruit of labeling is positive. You're trying to serve God and function in a way that honors fellowship while maintaining your character. The motivation is love . . . to serve God and to serve others with the right spirit.

---

8. Respond to this statement: **name calling** is about hurting, demeaning, and using words as a weapon but **labeling** is about understanding so we can change our tactics.

How can we be sure we are labeling for redemptive purposes and not name calling?

9. When we label and walk away from a toxic person, there are two things we are seeking to do. Describe what it will look like in your life when you are seeking to do each of these things:

When I am guarding my mission, I will . . .

To maintain my character, I need to . . .

10. How can your group members pray for you, encourage you, and support you as you seek to crystalize God's mission for you and as you maintain and grow character that looks like Jesus?

I can't control a toxic person. I can't change a toxic person. I can't even understand a toxic person. What I can do is guard my mission and maintain my character.

CLOSING PRAYER

Spend time in your group praying in some of the following directions:

- Lift up prayers of thanks that Jesus was a bold and clear truth-teller.

- Ask the Holy Spirit to give you discernment and clarity of thought so you can identify toxic behaviors and attitudes and speak truth against them.

- Pray for humility and care as you speak the truth to others so you will not become arrogant or inappropriately judgmental.

- Pray that you can see the truth, speak the truth, and then walk in the truth so that you can stay on mission and develop character that looks more and more like Jesus.

Jesus believes in truth telling.

BETWEEN-SESSIONS PERSONAL STUDY

Reflect on the content you've covered this week in *When to Walk Away* by engaging in any or all of the following between-sessions activities. The time you invest will be well spent, so let God use it to draw you closer to him. At your next meeting, share with your group any key points or insights that stood out to you as spent this time with the Lord.

KNOW THE DIFFERENCE

We need to be careful and prayerful before ever giving someone the label "toxic." But, if someone is clearly toxic, it is actually helpful and honoring to Jesus to give a label so they can be dealt with and do minimum damage to people, the church, and the name of Jesus. Take some time to clarify in your own mind the difference between "labeling" a person and "name calling." **Name calling** is intended to be hurtful; it is demeaning; and it is used as a weapon to hurt a person.

What are signs that you are "name calling"?

How can you keep from "name calling" and be careful you am not hurting others with such behavior?

Labeling gives a name to a sickness; it should be done carefully; it is about understanding; and it helps you change your tactics to protect others and yourself.

What are some situations when labeling is necessary?

How can I keep make sure "labeling" does not deteriorate into "name calling"?

---

*The fruit of **name calling** is destructive. It's about destroying someone's reputation. We should never call someone toxic to hurt them or injure their reputation with others. **Labeling** isn't name calling. It doesn't dishonor people when we speak truthfully.*

LEARNING FROM THE MASTER

During Jesus' ministry on earth, he used very positive titles and names for people that served to build them up. He also gave clear and precise warning labels for people who were toxic and dangerous. Take time to read the four Gospels this week, and then underline or highlight some times when Jesus gives an affirming and positive title to a person. Also, underline or highlight times Jesus labels someone. Use the tables on the next pages to to gather your observations.

POSITIVE TITLES / NAMES JESUS GAVE PEOPLE:

Passage	Who	Title given	Meaning
Matt. 16:18	Peter	Rock	You will be a strong leader, a foundational person

LABELS JESUS GAVE PEOPLE:

Passage	Who	Title given	Meaning
Matt. 23:33	Phari-sees	Snakes, vipers	They were poisonous, deadly, sneaky, deceptive

THE POWER OF BLESSING

Thankfully, in most of our lives, there are far more people who bless us, encourage us, and become a conduit of God's grace and kindness. As we learn to identify and walk away from toxic people, we are wise to remember and celebrate those who are the polar opposite of toxic. They are gracious, kind, and givers of life.

Take time to connect with a couple of these gracious and humble people by writing a note, email, or text, giving them a phone call, or finding a time to meet with them. Express, with as much clarity as you can, how God has used them in your life to bring blessing, joy, encouragement, and hope.

People I should connect with to thank and bless:

-
-
-
-
-
-
-
-
-
-
-
-
-
-
-

JOURNAL

Use the space provided below to write some reflections on the following topics:

- In what ways do I need to be more careful and cautious about possible "name calling"? Are there ways I have done this?

- If so, how can I repent and move away from this?

- Where do I need to be bolder and stronger so that I can "label" a toxic person and protect myself, others, the church, and the cause of Jesus?

RECOMMENDED READING

As you reflect on what God is teaching you through this session, you may want to read chapters 8 and 9 of *When to Walk Away: Finding Freedom from Toxic People.*

ALIGN WITH CHRIST

*Family ties and friendships are important. But, above all relationships, **our commitment to Jesus must come first.** When it does, we have the courage to walk away from any toxic relationship, no matter how close we are to the person.*

INTRODUCTION

Evan grew up among atheists. In his entire extended family there was only one Christian. So, when Evan became a follower of Jesus at age fifteen, his parents and siblings did not understand. They were not vicious at first. There were a lot of jokes, subtle taunts, and consistent comments about how "Evan will get over the whole Jesus thing eventually."

As the years passed, Evan showed no signs of leaving his faith behind. His faith grew deeper and his convictions shaped his lifestyle and actions. The jokes and gibes became more personal, more aggressive, and more frequent. With time his family began to unite around the mission of convincing Evan to jettison his Christianity and adopt a secular humanistic philosophy that was "more fitting a member of their family."

Evan found himself always on the defensive and continually under attack. It felt like he had to make some very serious decisions about where he would place his allegiance. His family was forcing him to choose them or Jesus.

When Jasmine married Malik, a committed follower of Christ, her own faith in Jesus (born in college) deepened considerably, much to the chagrin of Jasmine's family, who nominally ascribed to (but didn't actually practice) a different faith. They accused Malik of "brainwashing" Jasmine. Her siblings and even her dad loved using family gatherings to embarrass Jasmine by recounting, in front of Malik, all the colorful stories of Jasmine's past before she met Malik and before she started practicing her faith. Malik had learned how to navigate these family gatherings, but when he and Jasmine began having children, several family members took this opposition to a new level. They blatantly asked Malik if he planned on brainwashing his children like he had his wife.

As the years went by, two of Jasmine's family members became more serious about their own faith. Malik could tell by their side conversations with his children that they were intent on undercutting his children's belief in Jesus in favor of the faith of Jasmine's family. He heard them utter slurs against the Bible, such as, "Haven't your parents told you the Bible has been changed many times?" and, "How do you know the one they are giving you is the truth?" They even uttered slurs against Jesus, saying, "He may be a prophet, but if he was God, you'd have three deities—and there is only one God."

The moment of truth came when these family members asked Jasmine if her children could spend a week with them at a family camp. She knew her parents would be deeply offended if she didn't let her children go, but Malik was insistent this was just another ploy to destroy their children's faith in Jesus. Jasmine knew Malik was telling the truth. She realized she was going to have to make a choice between pleasing her parents or honoring her immediate family's faith in Christ.

Jesus was clear that sometimes faith and family will conflict. When this happens, faith always wins.

TALK ABOUT IT

Begin your group time by inviting anyone to share his or her insights from last week's personal study. Next, to kick things off, discuss one of the following questions:

- If you have experienced tension with family members because of your faith in Jesus, share how you have navigated this situation.

—or—

- What are some tensions and conflicts people experience when their faith in Jesus does not line up with the beliefs, norms, or culture of their family?

Jesus puts allegiance to his blood above familial blood.

TEACHING NOTES

As you watch the video teaching segment for this session, use the following outline to record any thoughts or concepts that stand out to you.

Angie's mother-in-law . . . passive-aggressive abuse

Family loyalty . . . can it become idolatrous?

Our commitment to Jesus . . . above all people and all things

Jesus and his family . . . keeping the mission first

Biblical examples . . . authority balanced by surrender to God's will

---

Jesus' willingness to walk away from his family while they resisted him, opened the door to their walking toward him after he rose from the dead.

Real-life examples . . . playing the "but I thought that you were a Christian" card

Healthy people . . . responding to the unhealthy people who are in our family

God is with us . . . even when others turn against us

---

*Ordering your life around serving God first
brings the stability of being affirmed, cared for,
protected, and comforted by a perfectly consistent,
unchanging, and loving heavenly Father.*

GROUP DISCUSSION

Take a few minutes with your group members to discuss what you just watched and explore these concepts in Scripture.

1. What would you say to a person who declares, with confidence, "The Bible says I have to honor my father and mother, so I can never act in a way that will upset them or go against what they want"? How is this quote from Exodus 20 (in the Ten Commandments), only part of the story when it comes to how we relate with family?

2. Read Matthew 10:34–39. What is the heartbeat of what Jesus is trying to say about the level of our allegiance to him versus our birth family or anyone else?

Take a moment and write one sentence summarizing what you think Jesus is seeking to teach his followers.

If you feel comfortable, read your sentence to your group and clarify what you believe Jesus is communicating to every person who claims him as their Savior and the leader of their life.

Allegiance to Jesus has to be so deep that any challenge is really no challenge at all.

---

3. **Read Luke 14:26–27.** If we read this passage with no context, what does it seem to be saying? If we read it in the context of all of Jesus' teaching and ministry, what is Jesus seeking to teach us?

4. Jesus calls his disciples to take up their cross and follow him. What does this language mean, and how does this image of cross bearing speak to our level of devotion to any person compared to our commitment to Jesus?

5. Read Matthew 12:46–50. How did Jesus model this commitment to the work of God's kingdom above all other things, including family? How do you need to learn from this example and put Jesus before your family?

6. Read Matthew 10:16–17 and Romans 16:17–18. Why do you think Jesus calls us to be both shrewd as snakes and innocent as doves? Give an example of what does it look like when we are doing both of these well. What kind of people is Paul warning us to avoid?

Both Jesus and Paul commend a combination of wisdom and innocence when dealing with evil people.

---

7. Read Romans 13:1 and Colossians 3:18–21. In the Bible we are taught to recognize and respect authority. But in each case, there is a counterbalance that makes it clear that there are limits to authority. If governmental or familial authority becomes toxic or dangerous, we are to press back against human authority and submit to God. What are examples of times when authority crosses the line and should no longer be honored?

8. What are some of the ways you have seen (or heard about) toxic people manipulating authority (in a home, work place, the church, or some other setting)? How can we push back, battle this manipulation, and walk away from these toxic settings?

We must be willing to look evil in the face and protect ourselves and those we love from it.

---

9. In this session we are encouraged to think about how we might talk more with our children, grandchildren, and young people about the reality of evil and our battle with Satan and toxic people. What are some pieces of advice that you could give to young people about what you have learned in this study that might save them a lot of heartache and pain in their future?

10. Read Isaiah 52:12 and Psalm 28:7. When we walk away from toxic people in our family, in social settings, and even in the church, we still have a source of support and encouragement that no one can ever take away. How does God uphold and support us when we are taking a stand and walking away from toxic people? Tell about how you experienced God's presence, power, and grace in a time when you had to separate from a toxic situation and person.

What are some of the practical ways we can support and care for other followers of Jesus when they need the support and love of God's family? How can you, as group members, fortify and encourage each other as you deal with toxic people in your life?

Breaking with a family member or having them reject us can feel crushing. If you have to travel that sad road, learn to find solace in your surest hope, you are not only losing a toxic earthly family, you are gaining a holy affirming heavenly family.

CLOSING PRAYER

Spend time in your group praying in some of the following directions:

- Thank God for family members who love Jesus and who cheer you on with their example or words as you follow the Savior.

- Pray for a heart that is so radically devoted to Jesus that all human allegiances pale in comparison.

- Ask the Spirit of the Living God to fill you with power to resist, draw lines, or even walk away from family members that are toxic and seeking to damage or destroy your faith.

- Pray for your group members, by name, as all of you seek to live a life devoted to Jesus and committed to invest your time and energy in faithful people who are hungry to grow in faith and eager to learn.

May God grant you many fruitful years of seeking first his kingdom and investing your life in reliable people to God's glory and good pleasure.

BETWEEN-SESSIONS PERSONAL STUDY

Reflect on the content you've covered during this final week in *When to Walk Away* by engaging in any or all of the following between-sessions activities. The time you invest will be well spent, so let God use it to draw you closer to him. Be sure to share with your group leader or group members in the upcoming weeks any key points or insights that stood out to you.

GOD IS MY STRENGTH!

Take time today to read and memorize one or two passages about how God is your protector, fortress, and stronghold. Let this truth fill your mind and heart any time you feel discouraged because you are dealing with a toxic person. Here are some examples:

> The LORD is my rock, my fortress and my deliverer; my God is my rock, in whom I take refuge, my shield and the horn of my salvation, my stronghold (Psalm 18:2).

> God is our refuge and strength, an ever-present help in trouble (Psalm 46:1).

> Have mercy on me, my God, have mercy on me, for in you I take refuge. I will take refuge in the shadow of your wings until the disaster has passed (Psalm 57:1).

MY STRATEGY FOR HELPING THE NEXT GENERATION

We are wise to teach young people about the reality of toxic people, the damage they do, and how we walk away from them or limit their power in our life. Take some time and prayerfully write down your best five truths from this study that you could teach to the next generation.

LESSONS I SHOULD TEACH CHILDREN
(7- TO 12-YEAR-OLDS)

LESSONS I SHOULD TEACH TEENS
(13- TO 17-YEAR-OLDS)

GOD ABOVE FAMILY

Take time to reflect on the implications if we put family first in our life above God. Write down some of the repercussions and consequences we might face if we live this way:

How will our family be impacted if we seek God first in our life and keep our faith in Jesus as the central hub around which everything else circles?

What are two or three specific and measurable actions you can take to make sure you are seeking God first in your life (home, heart, workplace, free time...)

JOURNAL

Use the space provided below to write some reflections on the following topics:

- Who is a reliable person God has placed in your life and how can you invest in this person's spiritual health and growth over the coming year?

- Who is a toxic person that is still infecting your life and discouraging your soul?

- What is your next step in walking away from this person's influence and impact on your life?

RECOMMENDED READING

As you reflect on what God is teaching you through this session, you may want to read chapters 13 and 14 of *When to Walk Away: Finding Freedom from Toxic People.*

LEADER'S GUIDE

Thank you for your willingness to lead your group through this study! What you have chosen to do is valuable and will make a great difference in the lives of others. The rewards of being a leader are different from those of participating, and we hope that as you lead you will find your own walk with Jesus deepened by this experience.

When to Walk Away is a six-session study built around video content and small-group interaction. As the group leader, just think of yourself as the host of a dinner party. Your job is to take care of your guests by managing all the behind-the-scenes details so that when everyone arrives, they can just enjoy time together.

As the group leader, your role is not to answer all the questions or reteach the content—the video, book, and study guide will do most of that work. Your job is to guide the experience and cultivate your small group into a kind of teaching community. This will make it a place for members to process, question, and reflect—not receive more instruction.

Before your first meeting, make sure everyone in the group gets a copy of the study guide. This will keep everyone on the same page and help the process run more smoothly. If some group members are unable to purchase the guide, arrange it so that people can share the resource with other group members. Giving everyone access to all the material will position this study to be as rewarding an experience as possible. Everyone should feel free to write in his or her study guide and bring it to group every week.

SETTING UP THE GROUP

You will need to determine with your group members how long you want to meet each week so you can plan your time accordingly. Generally, most groups like to meet for either ninety minutes or two hours, so you could use one of the following schedules:

Section	90 Minutes	120 Minutes
Welcome (members arrive and get settled)	10 minutes	15 minutes
Share (discuss one or more of the opening questions)	15 minutes	20 minutes
Watch (watch the teaching material and take notes)	25 minutes	25 minutes
Discuss (discuss the Bible study questions you selected)	30 minutes	45 minutes
Respond (pray together as a group and dismiss)	10 minutes	15 minutes

As the group leader, you'll want to create an environment that encourages sharing and learning. A church sanctuary or formal classroom may not be as ideal as a living room, because those locations can feel formal and less intimate. No matter what setting you choose, provide enough comfortable seating for everyone, and, if possible, arrange the seats in a semicircle so everyone can see the video easily. This will make transition between the video and group conversation more efficient and natural.

Also, try to get to the meeting site early so you can greet participants as they arrive. Simple refreshments create a welcoming atmosphere and can be a wonderful addition to a group study evening. Try to take food and pet allergies into account to make your guests as comfortable as possible. You may also want to consider offering childcare to couples with children who want to attend. Finally, be sure your media technology is working properly. Managing these details up front will make the rest of your group experience flow smoothly and provide a welcoming space in which to engage the content of *When to Walk Away*.

STARTING THE GROUP TIME

Once everyone has arrived, it's time to begin the group. Here are some simple tips to make your group time healthy, enjoyable, and effective.

First, begin the meeting with a short prayer and remind the group members to put their phones on silent. This is a way to make sure you can all be present with one another and with God. Next, give each person a few minutes to respond to the questions in the "Talk About It" section. This won't require as much time in session one, but beginning in session two, people will need more time to share their insights from their personal studies. Usually, you won't answer the discussion questions yourself, but you should go first with the "Talk About It" questions, answering briefly and with a reasonable amount of transparency.

At the end of session one, invite the group members to complete the between-sessions personal studies for that week. Explain that you will be providing some time before the video teaching next week for anyone to share insights. Let them know sharing is optional, and it's no problem if they can't get to some of the between-sessions activities some weeks. It will still be beneficial for them to hear from the other participants and learn about what they discovered.

LEADING THE DISCUSSION TIME

Now that the group is engaged, it's time to watch the video and respond with some directed small-group discussion. Encourage all the group members to participate in the discussion, but make sure they know they don't have to do so. As the discussion progresses, you may want to follow up with comments such as, "Tell me more about that," or, "Why did you answer that way?" This will allow the group participants to deepen their reflections and invite meaningful sharing in a nonthreatening way.

Note that you have been given multiple questions to use in each session, and you do not have to use them all or even follow them in order. Feel free to pick and choose questions based on either the needs of your group or how the conversation is flowing. Also, don't be afraid of silence. Offering a question and allowing up to thirty seconds of silence is okay. It allows people space to think about how they want to respond and also gives them time to do so.

As group leader, you are the boundary keeper for your group. Do not let anyone (yourself included) dominate the group time. Keep an eye out for group members who might be tempted to "attack" folks they disagree with or try to "fix" those having struggles. These kinds of behaviors can derail a group's momentum, so they need to be steered in a different direction. Model active listening and encourage everyone in your group to do the same. This will make your group time a safe space and create a positive community.

The group discussion leads to a closing time of individual reflection and prayer. Encourage the participants to take a few moments to review what they have learned during the session. This will help them tp cement the big ideas in their minds as you close. Conclude by praying together as a group.

GROUP DYNAMICS

Leading a group study can be a rewarding experience for you and your group members—but that doesn't mean there won't be challenges. Certain members may feel uncomfortable discussing topics that they consider personal and might be afraid of being called on. Some members might have disagreements on specific issues. To help prevent these scenarios, consider the following ground rules:

* If someone has a question that seems off topic, suggest that it be discussed at another time, or

you can ask the group members if they are okay with addressing that topic.

- If someone asks a question you don't know the answer to, confess that you don't know and move on. If you feel comfortable, invite other group members to give their opinions or share their comments based on personal experience.

- If you feel like a couple of people in the group are talking much more than others, direct questions to people who may not have shared yet. You could even ask the more dominating members to help draw out the quiet ones.

- When there is a disagreement, encourage the group members to process the matter in love. Invite members from opposing sides to evaluate their opinions and consider the ideas of the other members. Lead the group through Scripture that addresses the topic, and look for common ground.

When issues arise, encourage your group to follow these words from Scripture: "Love one another" (John 13:34), "If it is possible, as much as it depends on you, live peaceably with all men" (Romans 12:18), and, "Be swift to hear, slow to speak, slow to wrath" (James 1:19). This will make your group time more rewarding and beneficial for everyone who attends.

Thank you again for your willingness to lead your group. May God reward your efforts and make your time together in *When to Walk Away* fruitful for his kingdom.

When to Walk Away

Finding Freedom from Toxic People

Gary Thomas

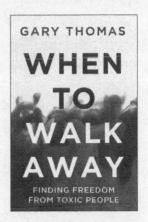

As Christians, we often feel the guilt and responsibility of meeting the needs of unhealthy people in our lives. Whether a sibling, parent, spouse, coworker, or friend, toxic people always seek to frustrate our life's calling. While you're seeking first God's kingdom, they're seeking first to distract your focus and delay your work.

Instead of attempting the impossible task of mollifying toxic people, it's time we dedicate our energy to the only worthwhile effort: completing the work God has given us. It's only when we learn to say no to bad patterns can we say yes to the good God has planned for us.

Gary Thomas, bestselling author of *Sacred Marriage*, looks at biblical examples from the lives of Jesus, Paul, and Nehemiah. Drawing from years serving as a pastor, Thomas shares modern stories and practical examples for dealing with the difficult people in our lives. Each chapter includes insightful take-aways that you can apply right away. You'll discover how to:

- Set healthy boundaries to protect your life's calling
- Find refuge in God when you feel under attack
- Discern when to walk away from a toxic situation
- Keep a tender heart even in unhealthy relationships
- Love and serve difficult people by resisting their control
- Grow your inner strength and invest in reliable people

We can't let others steal our joy or our mission. It's time to strengthen our defense, learn to set good boundaries, and focus on our God-given purpose.

Available in stores and online!

Discover a Deeper Intimacy with God Through Your Marriage

In this six-session small group Bible study, writer and speaker Gary Thomas invites you to see how God can use marriage as a discipline and a motivation to reflect more of the character of Jesus.

Your marriage is much more than a union between you and your spouse; it is a spiritual discipline ideally suited to help you know God more fully and intimately. *Sacred Marriage* shifts the focus from marital enrichment to spiritual enrichment in ways that can help you love your mate more. Whether it is delightful or difficult, your marriage can become a doorway to a closer walk with God.

Book	Participant's Guide	DVD
9780310337379	9780310880660	9780310352266

Available now at your favorite bookstore,
or streaming video on StudyGateway.com.